Island Lovers

Poems and Images
of Mauritius

COPYRIGHT © 2016 PEGGY LAMPOTANG

All rights reserved. No part of this publication may be reproduced or transmitted in any form or by any means, electronic, mechanical, photocopying, recording, or any information storage and retrieval system, without the prior consent of the publisher.

Layout by TPrinters Co. Ltd.
Cover design and photographs by Peggy Lampotang

All photographs by Peggy Lampotang

ISBN 978-0-9939942-1-0

Published in 2016 by Design 51 Inc.
Toronto - Canada

Printed by TPrinters Co. Ltd. in Mauritius
July 2016

Island Lovers

Poems and Images of Mauritius

Peggy Lampotang

To Mauritius, the island I left ...

Contents

Island Lovers   **8**

Forever Free   10
Island   12
The Deep Blue   14
Hope   16
Flux   18
Water   20
Waiting   22
Gris-Gris   24

Historical Musings   **26**

Vieux Grand Port   28
Tunnel of Shade   30
The Road to Albion   32
Gems   34
Signal Mountain   36
Salt   38
La Boutik   40

Island Nature   **42**

Fields of Light   44
Roots   46
Striated Heron   48
The Canopy Tree   50
Tortoise   52
Random Buds   54
Shack   56

Islanders   **58**

Captive   60
Friendship   62
The Shrine   64
Fisherman   66
At the Market   68
Echoes of the Past   70
The Kiss   72
Goodbye   74

Acknowledgements   77

Island Lovers

Forever Free

I am the swelling waves
that crash on your shore
pulling back and forth
leaving smashed debris
broken shells and foam

You're a sturdy island
firm, unmovable
while I whine, strike
recoil, rage, roll over
and rest on your lap

I spread my frilly skirt
on your staid shoreline
let it ripple, fizzle over
your tremulous sand
and withdraw, consumed

I reach your inner coast
stir your woody scent
soothe the prickly heat
of your dark fertile soil
leaving you soaked

I am the retreating waves
rumbling from your stillness
to flirt with other shores
forever free to roam
yet dashing back to you

Island

A distant rock, removed,
elusive, a fleeting mirage,
you linger on my horizon.

I danced in your verdant air,
cool blues, and rosy views,
weathered your fiery streaks,
melted in your gilded light.

Then heavy clouds loomed,
laden with constraints,
pouring endless chatter
till I wilted in your rain.

Revived on fresh new soil,
creative shoots blooming,
I remember seeds sown
in your remote splendour.

You linger on my horizon,
a fleeting mirage, elusive,
removed, a distant rock.

The Deep Blue

You are the sea
heaving with danger
simmering
beneath
my steady boat
you lure me with
the rhapsody
of your surging crests
I want to plunge
into the gush
of your effusion
and try oh so hard
to grasp the comfort
of your turbulence
I hear the wind
whispering
enticing me
to gloss over
your treacherous depth
I throw my heart
it skips across
your body of water
one - two - three
I tumble down
sink and sink
into the deep blue
searching for
the real you

Hope

I was lost and grey
an ocean filled with tears

from the dark clouds
a shaft of light broke free

silver slivers of hope
twinkled on the surface

and my forlorn heart
glided with equanimity

bearing no fear
towards uncertainty

Flux

Angry waves charge
onto the rocky shore,
sting, drench my bare feet.
They reel back, reckless,
bashing louder, furious,
whipping harder, rougher.
I don't heed their assault
and they hiss, hit me again
till I cry out, broken.

Gentle waves lull me
into a blissful trance.
I float on the rubber mat,
undulating to the cadence,
aching with love,
summer juices spilling
from the fruits in my mouth,
the sun burning my skin
as I splash water to cool off.

Waves of grief and rapture in flux,
fervour diminished with time
in a tranquil ebb and flow, but
can wisdom subdue passion?

Water

You are the water
that quenches my thirst
but I keep craving more

You coast along
fluid, undefined, non-committal
murmurs of shed lives
echo in your warbles

You are the water
I cup in my hand
but you drip between my fingers

Waiting

There's an empty seat for you
with promises of brighter days

See the light through the leaves
their transparent filigreed veins
fragile within clear sheaths
glowing, radiant with life
waiting for you to find your way
before dusk slides into darkness

Come before the leaves have shed
gnarled, withered, come my love

Gris-Gris

Sitting on the southern edge of the island
hearts pounding with each roaring crash

lovers mesmerized by rhythmic violence
unrestrained fury, yet serene from release

a moment of calm replenishes souls
from the terror of the unknown

they hold each other, lost in their smallness
for no land lies from here to Antarctica

Historical Musings

Grand Port

The lion reigned unfazed over the ocean
when sailors disembarked from arduous voyages,
thrilled to find an oasis flowing with palm trees,
where they filled up with spring water and coconuts.

It did not roar when the Dutch settled in 1638,
depleting the island of ebony trees for exportation,
but let cyclones, rodent infestations dishearten them
till they deserted, after eating Dodo birds to extinction.

It did not growl in 1715 as the French sailed in,
raising their flag to claim the land as Isle de France,
undeterred by foul weather or pests, dragging slaves
from Africa to plough sugarcane fields, build houses.

In 1810, it shuddered from British cannons,
a bloody battle waged to control this useful
port of call at the heart of the Indian Ocean
for lucrative trade between England and India.

It basked under the light of freedom in 1968
when the restless nation asserted its autonomy,
energized by its resourceful mix of immigrants
from France, Africa, Britain, India and China.

The lion reigns unfazed over the ocean
when tourists descend from airplanes, snap photos
of the leonine shape guarding the port, restful
as it stands the test of time, transcends history.

Tunnel of Shade

It is said that Napoleon ordered trees
planted on both sides of rural streets
to protect his army from the blistering sun,
leaving corridors of green canopies
along the rolling French countryside.

Those tunnels of lacy foliage were perhaps
recreated by nostalgic French colonists
on this tropical isle, their little France,
roads not for their emperor, towards Rome
but a prosperous sanctuary from home.

Now vehicles whir by on ribbons of shade
trees stand at attention, passengers refreshed
before the sun blazes anew on paths laid
by these conquerors, their legacy woven
throughout a paradise they now call home.

The Road to Albion

Albion, the rustic town's name, reminder
of a time when Britain ruled our island
and we believed our skin should be whiter
so we could take tea and biscuits on verandahs
with creamy lacy trim and wicker chairs.

We enunciated English words, shunned Creole,
knew more about the Wars of the Roses
than our slave rebellions or Grand Port Battle,
studied poems of Blake, Shelley and Wordsworth,
unaware of Edouard Maunick, Jean Georges Prosper.

Albion, expanding coastal town boasting
white houses with blue corrugated roofs,
tree-lined streets that lead to the sea towards
the other Albion, parent country that kept us docile
yet gave us education and democracy.

O perfidious old Albion, you granted independence
we yearned for, but kept Chagos, our outer island,
forced a nation's exile for Americans' military base,
the deal, a shame that keeps burning in the forest
of our conscience as we try to claim back the land.

Albion, the rustic town's name, reminder
of a time when Britain ruled our island
but now we take tea and biscuits on verandahs,
proud to speak Creole, and worship local poets,
our skin shining in harmonious shades.

Gems

There's a fire across the sky,
its embers turning to ash,
shrouding a smoldering night
flush with hidden secrets.

Legends tell that pirates,
laden with loot, gained shelter
on this isle where they perished,
clutching their doubloons.

It is said that stolen gems,
buried with ravaged bodies,
will unleash their curse
if ever disinterred.

Covetous of these riches,
many hunt for skeletons,
dig under the cloak of twilight,
and mysteriously disappear.

Blind to the sapphire sky,
deaf to the ruby birds' trill,
numb to the emerald trees
and the tang of the turquoise sea.

Signal Mountain

A volcanic mound soaring above the harbour,
a sentinel watching settlers tame an uninhabited
land overtaken with vegetation and wild birds.

It has stood steadfast against raging cyclones,
trade winds, erosion, while newcomers toiled,
turning a sprinkling of houses into a packed town.

On its peak, revellers have blasted fireworks
into the night, exploding colours of joy,
jubilation for wars won, freedom gained.

Now, it gazes at buildings jutting into the sky,
its relay station high atop, flashing signals,
blinking at its impact on rapid advances.

It's been scarred by paths carved through its flanks
for hikers clambering the slope at dawn and dusk,
exalted as they merge with the celestial infinity.

In the night's shadow, bewitched by jewelled lights,
scintillating sea, the guardian emanates warmth,
constant through incessant changes, a beacon.

Salt

Ocean water glimmers under the sun
evaporates, leaving crystals

swept into mounds in saltpans
minerals fit for consumption

to season, enhance, preserve
sustain us through centuries

prized, bartered, battled over
iodized, processed for profits

the common zest loses its allure
workers' livelihoods threatened

but gourmets discern the ocean
aroma of wooden-raked fleur de sel

flavours from distinct harvests
ensure sea salt tradition lives on

La Boutik

In earlier times, the shopkeeper served villagers
in la boutik, a community refuge, warm aroma
of fresh baked bread wafting above waxy odours
of Gossage soaps, sharp scent of chili pepper,
assuaging hardships, hunger, with rice, lentils,
salted fish, offering credit to barefoot workers
who saunter to sugarcane fields, rolling cigarettes,
sighing as they exhale longings into the dewy dawn.

As the island prospers, supermarkets' widespread
tentacles strangle shops one by one, shopkeepers'
children break out of the mold into novel spheres
yet la boutik subsists, a few owners, doors open,
fill villagers' needs, their profusion of eclectic goods,
communal friendliness redolent of bygone days.

Of Nature

Fields of Light

A silver tipped field of flowering sugarcanes
billows in the wind on a luminous day
but is it the sun
or the blossoms
that exude such radiance?

Are the plants spurting light from their feathery bloom
or have our eyes, dazzled by
shimmering tassels,
endowed them
with our mystical elation?

Roots

Intrepid limbs crawl, curl
out of the soil into daylight,
meander, twist around the tree
they built, flaunt in the open
a dense tangle of complex ties,
chaotic uprising mocking rules,
naked exposure, a new reckoning,
sunlight coursing down their core,
altering earth's expectations.

Striated Heron

Softly on the pad it treads
to strike at a water strider

Eagerly it swallows its prey
and clucks with contentment

Its simple life a flitting arc
the lily pond its green planet

The Canopy Tree

It awaits, extends its arms, a wistful sigh
of breezy leaves draws us to patio chairs
where we laze in its majestic shade
bemused creatures sipping rum
drunk with the humid scent of earth
basking in the illusory permanence of safety
we scoff at mortality with a shot of good cheer
indolent summer days dampening our will
prolonging delusions, but why not we say
for life's short and tomorrow's another day

Tortoise

It holds silence
in its leathery skin
like a sage wizened
by cruel weather
sustains the weight
of bouncing children
on its hardened shell
unperturbed
by fast-paced visitors
it plods its path
sniffs knowledge
at an even pace
outlives them all

Random Buds

Wind-strewn seeds blossom through trash
burrow their sturdy roots through cracked walls
for tired eyes to marvel at the savage beauty
of wild flowers cascading in exuberant fuchsia
their melodious shapes softening hard edges
murmuring sweet nothings to ailing souls
a spark of promise from a random bud

Shack

Scraps of corrugated metal
shelter from brutal elements
patchwork of deprivation
inventive outlet of chance artists
construction of would-be engineers
solution to shield few possessions
blown away by cyclones
rebuilt against the wind

Islanders

Captive

We are born to the song of rolling waves
our feet toughened on corals crushed to sand

We search the sea for bait, trap little lives
in clear bottles, gaze at their futile struggle

We're children of an island bound by an ocean
that holds us captive with its treasures

Friendship

Do you remember those sweltering days
discussing, dissecting love, friendship, men,
chatting till our minds blurred into a daze,
suffused with ideas that we, demure women,
embroidered, complicated into a maze
from which we shaped our haven?

What stories our naïve longings crafted
as we, sea-locked, let our rambling vision
rove, pollinate, breed with hopes lifted
on oppressive days of heat, torpid isolation,
to foreign places, emancipation, we drifted
our impossible dreams a fevered solution.

The Shrine

We march up the hill
for spiritual peace
from priests at the top
of Reine de la Paix
in the searing heat
parasols cooling
heavy feet aching
we repent our faults
replete with goodwill
easing daily grind
till back on the hill

Fisherman

A lone silhouette against the ocean
he casts his line, unruffled by
sailboats, intent on his catch
attuned to the shallow calm
he waits for a tug
of hook on flesh
for his hand to grip
a slippery fish,
quiet its spastic fight
in the setting sun's gold-lit embrace
each death another's sustenance
in the ceaseless cycle of renewal

At the Market

In the blue morning haze
beneath his pensive gaze
shadows of his past unfold
with hardships never told
alone among familiar faces
his own world to behold

Echoes of the Past

I choose to twirl my skirt
to sway, spin, slide,
sega dance away bygones
sweat off bitter thoughts
cleanse, purge, erase
raw slashes scarred smooth

Yet echoes of the past rustle
through the swishing cloth
flap against my thigh
insistently pounding
in the beat of my feet
in the throb of my veins

The Kiss

An offer of warmth
to bridge the chasm
softly shyness hovers
a breath, a whisper
an offer of peace

Goodbye

Enthused smiles from passers-by
waving under sultry skies
sparks crackling in spirited debates
on busy streets, along beaches
velvety sand under our feet
fragrance of cumin at the bazar
hot chili fritters that melt in the mouth
sensory images that linger
as we fly back to distant lands

Acknowledgements

Many thanks

to all the people who appear in the photos,

Philip Lim whose talent in telling stories through the lens spurred my passion for photography,

Maty Grosman, Brigid Higgins, Michael MacConnell, Gregory Monteith, Susan Noakes, Ann Walmsley,
accomplished writers and friends whose edit helped to make these poems better,

Catherine Curr, my artist friend for her creative input on the images,

all the kind friends and relatives who drove me to inspiring places
in Mauritius and Rodrigues to take photos.

All photos were taken on the island of Mauritius
except for Tortoise and At the Market, which were taken in Rodrigues,
an autonomous outer island of the Republic of Mauritius.

Website: peggylampotang.com
Blog: peglam.blogspot.com

COPYRIGHT © 2016 PEGGY LAMPOTANG